The Average Joe's Guide

to the Kindle Fire

by

Scott Hansen

TABLE OF CONTENTS

Preface

If you purchase this book you most likely have already purchased a Kindle Fire. Congratulations. This book is designed to help you get the most out of your new Kindle. Unlike a user manual, this book will be easy to read and easy to understand and it will help you become proficient when you go to use your Kindle Fire.

The first chapter will highlight the differences between the other Kindle products and the other e-readers on the market. The rest of the book will concentrate exclusively on the Kindle Fire and all of its functions.

This book is written for people who are not very tech-savvy or who do not have the time to figure out every little nuance of their new purchase. It is written for the average Joe or Josephine. When I sat down to write this book I tried to write it for my mom because if she can understand the terms and context in this book, then everyone should be able to grasp the knowledge presented.

Finally I want to thank Julie Sturek for giving me use of her photography talents. All photos in this book, including the cover, were taken by Julie. Julie's website is at http://thatmomentfrozen.com. Use this page to contact her and use her exceptional services. You can also email her at Julie@thatmomentfrozen.com.

1. Which Kindle is best for you?

There are a lot of e-readers out on the market and a lot of different tablets that can emulate an e-reader in the functionality. With all the competition out there, why purchase the Kindle Fire? There is no right or wrong answer to this question; there are simply pros and cons to every device out there on the market. The Kindle Fire is one option, albeit a very nice option, in a crowded marketplace.

The Kindle Fire is the newest offering in the Kindle product line. All previous versions of the Kindle readers are dedicated only to e-books and the screens are not in color. The print uses the new E Ink Pearl technology and offers a font that is easy to read, looks like it was printed on a piece of paper, and has no glare when you read these devices in direct sunlight. The other Kindles are priced from $79 to $379 as of this writing and each of these units offers something different in the reading experience.

If you are looking ONLY to read books on the device you purchase then the Kindle readers, not the Kindle Fire, are the products you should research and purchase. They are the top-of-the-line when it comes to functionality as well as having the power and strength of Amazon behind each sale.

Info: **All Kindles except the Kindle Fire have E Ink Pearl technology. All models except the DX have a 6" screen. You can get a new book downloaded in about one minute. All models allow you to select the text size displayed. All come with Amazon's cloud back up service and all have access to thousands of free books.**

The Kindle has no audio (this is important if you want speech to text capabilities), and no 3G connection, which means that you have to be in a Wi-Fi hot spot in order to download new books for your Kindle. This Kindle is NOT a touch screen model and you will have to scroll through pages using the handy buttons on the side of the model or the five way controller. This model has 2 GB of memory and can hold 1,400 books. This model has about 1 month of battery life.

The Kindle Touch comes in a Wi-Fi model, and a free 3G model, which allows you to download books in almost any country in the world for free. This Kindle has a touch screen to navigate through the device and it has audio output. It has 4 GB of memory and holds about 3,000 books. This model has about 2 months of battery life if the wireless is turned off.

The Kindle Keyboard comes in a Wi-Fi model and a free 3G model, which allows you to download books in almost any country in the world for free. This Kindle has a keyboard, buttons on the side of the device and a five way controller to access the content. It also has audio output. It has 4 GB of memory and holds about 3,500 books. This model has about 2 months of battery life if the wireless is turned off.

The Kindle DX has a 9.7" screen and is much larger than the other Kindle models. It weighs about 10 ounces more than all the other Kindle models. This Kindle has a keyboard, buttons on the side of the device and a five way controller to access the content. This item has a speaker for audio output. It has 4 GB of memory and holds about 3,500 books. This model has about 3 weeks of battery life if the wireless is turned off.

The Kindle Fire is the distant cousin in the Kindle family in that it is much more than just an e-reader. It has a bright and vivid color screen, which means it is not quite as good a reader as the other Kindle products. If you try to read a book in direct sunlight with this Kindle you will have glare on the screen and the sun might wash out the display, meaning you cannot read it on the beach.

However, this Kindle comes with the Silk internet web browser. The battery lasts for 8 hours if you are reading or 7.5 hours if you are watching videos. You can access videos on this Kindle and you can install apps that are designed for the Kindle. It has 8GB of memory and access to the Amazon Cloud for your offline storage. It can hold 80 apps plus 10 movies as well as 800 songs or 6,000 books. It weighs about 16 ounces so it weighs less that the DX, but more than the other Kindle products. It behaves much like the Apple iPad or any other tablet out on the market but with limited functionality. This Kindle was designed to work with Amazon products and the

Amazon cloud and it does it all very well.

2. Kindle and Amazon basics

Purchasing your Kindle Fire

The Kindle Fire can be purchased at most electronics stores like Best Buy or at office supply stores like Staples, Office Max or Office Depot. Target has discontinued their relationship with Kindle so you will not find them there. Going to a brick and mortar store has its advantages in that you can feel the different Kindles in your hand and you can see exactly how the device looks and feels to you. The other benefit from buying it at a regular brick and mortar store is instant gratification.

The Kindle Fire can also be purchased online from www.amazon.com and if you purchase Amazon Prime you will get your Kindle in two days. When you purchase your Kindle Fire from www.amazon.com they will load your Amazon account information into the Kindle before they ship it, which means when you turn the device on it will automatically connect you to Amazon.

Amazon Prime

If you decide to purchase the Kindle Fire from Amazon you may want to consider purchasing a membership to Amazon Prime. The first month of Amazon Prime is free and with Amazon Prime you get several benefits, including free 2 day shipping on any Amazon purchases, access to free e-books through the Kindle Lending Library each month, free movies, TV shows and other web content streamed instantly to your Kindle Fire or any other web-enabled device. The cost is minimal, at this writing it is $79 a year. I have found that Kindle Prime is well worth the money you will spend on the membership and my membership has paid for itself many times over.

Other Accessories to Consider

I would strongly recommend you purchase a couple of accessories with your Kindle Fire. These accessories will help protect your

Kindle from the elements and minor scratches for years to come. These accessories are not needed, but they do help protect the new look of your Kindle Fire.

Screen protector. Some writers say you do not need to purchase a screen protector because the screen on the Kindle Fire is made with Gorilla Glass, which is highly scratch resistant and a very sturdy product. If you do decide to purchase a screen protector then there are a couple of different manufacturers out there. If you read the reviews on www.amazon.com you will see that most all screen protectors get good reviews. Two popular brands are Zagg and Armorsuit. Both are good choices and it is very easy to get these items from www.amazon.com if you purchase your Kindle online.

A screen protector will help keep your Kindle touch screen clean and relatively fingerprint free. If you do get prints on the screen they are easy to wipe off and keep clean. It is important that if you buy a screen protector that you put it on as soon as possible so as not to trap in any stray dirt or hairs between the screen and the protective cover.

Some screen protectors have to sit for 24 hours after you apply them in order to adhere correctly to the Kindle. If you purchase the screen protector immediately it will help you keep your hands off the Kindle once you install it.

When you put your screen protector on the device, make sure that the bottom of the device is facing you and that the top of the Kindle Fire is facing away from you. The bottom of your Kindle is where the on and off button is located as well as the USB slot to hook up your charger. You will notice when you purchase a screen protector that the top left corner is notched, and this is to keep the ambient light sensor uncovered.

A Kindle case. I prefer a leather case for my Kindle. Leather looks good, it smells good, and it feels a lot less man-made than plastics. However, if you look online at Amazon you will find many different kinds of cases made out of many different types of materials. Whatever case you purchase is your decision. Either way, a case will protect your Kindle device from scratches and dirt and grime.

I found a case I liked on www.amazon.com and then I used www.google.com to Google the name of the case. If you do this click on shopping, and then sort by price to find the cheapest place to purchase the case. This is one of the few times I found prices significantly cheaper than if I purchased from Amazon.

The Amazon Basics USB Cable. Purchase this if you want to transfer files from your computer to your Amazon Kindle. The link for this is here: http://www.amazon.com/gp/product/B003ES5ZSW/ref=cm_cr_asin _lnk. Most users will not need or ever use a USB cable with their Kindle Fire.

Setting up an Amazon Account

When you purchase your Kindle fire you will want to set up an Amazon account if you do not already have one. This account will be your gateway to the Amazon Cloud where books, magazines, music, and other programs are stored for you. This will free up space on your Kindle Fire. If you sign up for Amazon Prime, this account will allow you to access the Kindle Lending Library and it will allow you to view and download all of the free TV shows and movies. You can also purchase movies to view.

Go to www.amazon.com and click on the "New customer? Start here" link. Enter your email address in the box provided and then click on the "No, I am a new customer" radio button. Click on the "Sign in using our secure server" button.

Fill out your name, retype your email address, enter your birthday and then select a secure password.

If you are going to purchase your Kindle from Amazon or sign up for Amazon Prime, you will have to give Amazon your credit card information. I have them keep this information on hand so I never have to look for my credit card when I place an order. From www.amazon.com you can search for books, magazines, shows, or movies that may interest you for your Kindle, as well as most any other product you are looking to purchase.

Remember, if you purchase Amazon Prime you will get free 2 day shipping on anything you order from Amazon. There is no minimum amount to purchase and the majority of products sold on Amazon come with this deal.

3. Your New Kindle Fire

Whether you purchase your Kindle Fire online or through a regular brick and mortar store, you will notice that the Kindle comes packaged in a brown Amazon box designed specifically for this product. It is slim and sleek and contains minimum waste. When you open the box you will find the Kindle Fire and a charger that plugs into an electrical outlet. That is it. There are no instructions except for one white card found in the lid of the box. Don't let this deter you; the rest of the setup is easy.

Figure The Kindle Fire out of the box.

Setting up your Kindle Fire on for the First Time

The on and off button is located on the bottom of your Kindle Fire. To turn on your Kindle Fire simply push the on/off button and release it. The on/off button will turn green. A couple of seconds will pass and the Kindle Fire logo will appear on the screen. It takes about 20-30 seconds for the Kindle Fire to boot up for the first time.

Once the main screen appears you will see a wallpaper background. There is one main slide bar in the middle of the screen with the current time and date. Use your finger to slide the yellow arrow from right to left, to unlock the welcome screen. To slide the bar, hold your finger on the yellow arrow banner and slide your finger across the screen from the right side to the left.

When you turn the Kindle for the first time a list of all available wireless networks will appear on the screen, usually sorted by the best Wi-Fi signal to the weakest. Find your Wi-Fi network and select it. Enter your password in the box provided if you set up your Wi-Fi network in the password protected mode. After you type in your password, hit the "connect" button to access your Wi-Fi network.

Once you initially connect to your home Wi-Fi network, you will automatically connect to the internet every time you turn on your Kindle Fire. You will not have to repeat this step unless you take your Kindle Fire away from home and have to find other wireless networks.

Next, set your time zone. The default is Pacific Time which is where Amazon headquarters is located.

If you purchase your Kindle Fire from www.amazon.com and you have an account set up with them, Amazon programs the Kindle Fire to access your Amazon account automatically. This means you do not need to type in your email address or your password. Amazon also assigns a name to your Kindle, but if you do not like the generic name they choose for you, then you can change the name of your Kindle Fire. The initial set up of the Kindle Fire is one very nice benefit to purchasing a Fire from Amazon.

At this time you will automatically register the device with Kindle. It may download some firmware, which is a software update for the Kindle Fire, but this download and install would be automatic. After this process completes your Kindle is set up and ready to go!

Whispersync and Whispernet

If you own more than one Kindle device you can read a book on both of the Kindles you own. Whispersync is an application that Amazon developed that will synchronize your devices when it comes to books. Whispersync will synchronize the devices so that your book marks and the page you last read will be the same across devices.

If you do not want to synchronize your devices, go to the <u>Manage Your Kindle</u> page on Amazon.com. In the left hand column under the heading "Your Kindle Account" there is a link that reads "Manage Your Devices." Click on this link and then scroll down under your devices to turn the Whispersync on or off.

Whispernet is NOT available on the Kindle Fire. On some Kindle models you can download books from anywhere in the United States, and in many foreign countries, without having to be near a Wi-Fi hot spot. Amazon created the Whispernet technology to deliver books or apps via cell phone carriers to the Kindle. With the Kindle Fire you absolutely need to be near a Wi-Fi hot spot to download books or content on your Kindle Fire.

Turning the Kindle on or off

The on/off button on the Kindle fire is on the bottom of the device. Push it once and immediately release the button to turn your device on. If your device was in sleep mode the home screen will appear almost immediately. If your device was turned off completely, then the Kindle Fire will need to boot up and this process can take anywhere from 20-30 seconds to complete.

Figure The Kindle Fire On/Off Button

There are two different modes when turning your device off.

Sleep mode: If you push the button once and immediately release it, the Kindle Fire will turn off but go into sleep mode. This means the next time you turn your Kindle on, it will not need to boot up. Your home screen will appear almost immediately and you will be able to use the slide bar function to access your Kindle Fire.

Shut down mode: If you want your Kindle to completely shut down, press the on/off button and hold it for a few seconds until a screen appears with two touch buttons on the screen. Your options are to either "Shut Down" or "Cancel." Select "Shut Down" if you want to completely turn off your device.

The Touch Screen

The Kindle Fire comes with a touch screen, there are no buttons used to navigate through the device. The touch screen is very responsive and if you have never used a touch screen it could take some getting used to. To unlock the device once it boots up you will simply place your finger in the yellow arrow section of the screen and then slide your finger from the right side of the screen to the left. The screen reacts to the touch from your fingers.

To turn pages in a book it is somewhat like turning the pages in a magazine or book. You place your finger anywhere on the right hand side of the screen and you slide your finger across the screen to the left, the same type of movement you would use holding a physical book. After a while you will become very adept and using the touch screen and it will be second nature to you.

If you are reading pages on the web and the text or photos are too small, you can zoom in on anything by touching the screen with your thumb and forefinger touching each other and the screen. Slide you thumb and forefinger slowly apart to zoom in on any area of text. When you have zoomed in you can move around the screen by putting your finger on the screen and dragging it to the part of the screen you want to read.

To zoom back out on the page or screen simply reverse the actions above. Place your finger and thumb on the screen but this time they will be apart, and while touching the screen bring your finger and thumb together, in a pinching motion. This action will zoom out in your document or on the web.

The zoom feature will NOT work when you play videos or read books.

You will also need to get used to touching icons on the screen to get into programs. Sometimes you will need to hold your finger down to complete an action, sometimes you will need to give the screen a double tap to perform an action. Different programs will require different input to perform an action. Much like playing Solitaire when you got your first computer helped improve your mouse skills, playing games on your Kindle Fire will help you learn and master how to use the touch screen.

Charging your Kindle Fire

Your Kindle Fire comes with a charger that plugs into an outlet in your home. On every screen of the Kindle Fire you will see an icon in the upper right hand corner that represents the battery life left in the device.

The Kindle will warn you with a pop-up button when you have only 15% of battery life remaining. If you are using the device and it runs out of juice, the Kindle will simply shut down. You will not hurt your Kindle Fire by letting it run out of power.

To recharge the battery plug the USB end into the bottom of the device and plug the other end into a wall outlet.

When you are charging your Kindle Fire the on/off button will be orange when the charging process is in progress. When the charge is complete the on/off button will change its color to green.

4. The Kindle Homepage

For future references in this book, the main screen on your Kindle will be referred to as the Kindle Homepage. On the Kindle homepage there are four main sections and each one performs a specific task or function. Once you get to know the desktop you will find it extremely intuitive to use.

Before we discuss the Kindle Homepage we will describe the icons that are located on the bottom of most Kindle screens. I call these the Frequently Used Icons.

Figure The Kindle homepage

Frequently used icons

At the bottom of most screens on the Kindle fire are the most important icons you will use. These icons will help you navigate from most every screen when you are using your Kindle. These icons are not visible on the home screen but are on most every other screen you will use when you use your Kindle. These icons are the home icon, the left arrow, the menu icon, and the magnifying glass icon.

The Home icon: Looks like a drawing of a house. This icon will bring you back to the Kindle homepage whenever you push this icon.

Figure The Home Icon.

The Back Arrow icon: This icon is used to back up a page. If you want to back to a previous page or previous pages, simply tap on this icon to bring you back one page. Depending on how deep you are into any one menu system, this icon will keep appearing until you finally reach the home page Kindle desktop.

Figure The Back Arrow Icon

The Menu icon: This icon looks like a piece of paper with lines written on it. When you press this icon you will get menu options specific to whatever program or page you happen to be viewing at the time. For instance, if you are in an app and you push this icon button you will most likely be given options or settings that can be set within the application you are using.

If you push this icon button in the Newsstand section, for instance, you will get the option of looking at the items on your Newsstand in either Grid or List view.

The menu icon is dependent on which screen or app you happen to be using at the time the icon button is pushed.

Figure The Menu Icon

The Search icon: This looks like a magnifying glass and this icon will bring up the search window and will allow you to search your Kindle for programs or specific magazines or newspapers that are available to you.

Figure The Search Icon

The different screen sections on your Kindle Fire home page.

There are four distinct sections that make up the Kindle Fire homepage. From the top of your Kindle to the bottom these sections are:

Section one is the top section on the Kindle screen and contains general information about the Kindle Fire. This section is represented by a thin line that contains your Kindle Fire device name, the current time, the settings icon, the Wi-Fi signal icon, and the battery level icon.

The second section looks like the menu bar to any Windows program. From this section you can access the Newsstand, Books, Music, Video, Docs, Apps, and the Web. Simply tap on any one of these items to access the various content within the sub menus.

The third section is called the Carousel. The Carousel contains all the recent items you have used or opened. It can contain icons representing apps, web browsing, books or magazines.

The fourth and final section is your favorites and this section can be as big or as small as you want it to be. If your favorite programs or icons take up a lot of space, then you will be able to scroll down on the desktop to see more shelves that contain your favorite icons. Kindle Fire simply builds another shelf on the book case if you add more favorites.

Section one of the home page

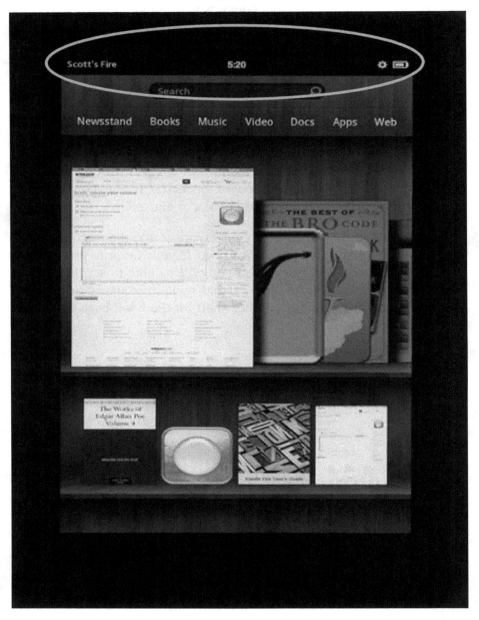

Figure Section One of the Home Page

Section one: The top section of the home page contains general information about your kindle as well as access to the setting menu. This section contains three distinct pieces of information: your device name, the time, and the settings, Wi-Fi and battery status.

Your Device Name: On the left will be your Kindle device name. If you order from Amazon they will create the device name for you. If you purchased your Kindle from a brick and mortar store you can give your device a name during the set up process.

If you want to change your device name you must go to www.amazon.com and log into your account. Towards the upper right hand part of the web page there is a tab labeled "Your Account." From the drop down menu select "Manage your Kindle." On the "Manage Your Kindle" page on the left hand side of the screen you will see "Manage your Devices" in the box labeled "Your Kindle Account." Next to the name of your Kindle device you will see an "Edit" link. Click this to change your device name and when you go to your Kindle you will notice the changes.

Next to your name you may see a circle with a number in it. If you touch the area with your name and there is a circle with a number in it, you will see notifications from Amazon. These read like emails and there is a button to clear out the messages if you are not interested in reading their alerts.

The Time: This section is in the center of the top section on the screen and it displays the time. You cannot access any other information here. If you touch this part of the screen nothing will happen.

The Settings Menu: This section is in the top right hand corner of the Kindle homepage screen. It contains an icon that looks like a gear, a symbol that looks like a tornado which is your Wi-Fi signal strength, and an icon representing how much power is left in the battery.

When you touch this section of the home screen it brings up the settings menu. The settings screen will be discussed in the next chapter.

Section two of the home page

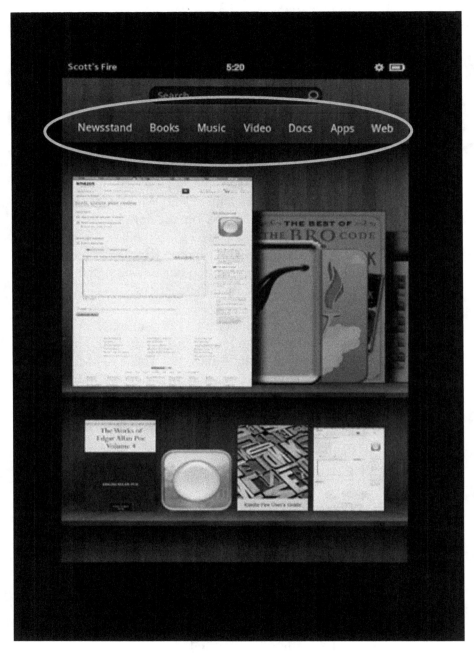

Figure Section Two of the Home Page

The next section of the home page contains a search window and tabs that will show you the different types of content that is available to your Kindle. The options are: Newsstand, Books, Music, Video, Docs, Apps, and Web.

Newsstand: If you select Newsstand a new screen will appear that will list all of your newspapers or magazines that you subscribe to on your bookshelf. On the top of this screen there are two different book shelves you can look at, the Cloud or the Device. If you select the Cloud tab your bookshelf will display all of the Newsstand content that is being saved on the internet for you. If you select the Device tab then the bookshelf will display all of the Newsstand items that have been downloaded to your Kindle Fire.

There is also a "Store" button at the top of this screen on the right. If you touch this you will be brought to the Amazon Newsstand store where you can purchase newspapers or magazines that you may be interested in.

If you have purchased a lot of newspapers or magazines your bookshelf will be full. To see ALL the titles on your bookshelf you can slide your finger from the bottom of the screen to the top to scroll up and see all your bookshelves.

Books: The Books option will bring up a list off all your books that you own displayed on a virtual bookshelf. When you select this option you can either look at the books that are located on the cloud or your device. You need to download books you want to read to your device in order to read them.

If you have a book that is on the cloud and not yet installed on your device, it will have an arrow pointing down next to the book name telling you that it needs to be downloaded to your device. When you tap on the book cover icon the Kindle will start downloading the book to your Fire.

To select a book to read, make sure that the "device" tab is selected on top and then simply tap on the icon of the book cover. This will open the book and you can navigate using the swiping motion to turn pages. If you are done reading a book and want to remove it from your device (but NOT remove it from the cloud) then tap and hold down your finger on the cover of the book. When you do this you are presented with two options, either you can "Add to Favorites" or "Remove from Device."

Reading books will be covered later in this book.

Music: Your Kindle Fire is a music player as well as an e-reader. You can either purchase your music from www.amazon.com or you can upload music to the Amazon Cloud that you already own. To upload your music, visit www.cloudplayer.com and follow the instruction there. Managing your music will be covered in a later chapter.

Video: The Kindle Fire was designed to integrate with the Amazon video service. If you sign up for Amazon Prime you will have access to hundreds, if not thousands, of free movies and TV shows that you can watch on your Kindle Fire or even watch on your T.V. if your T.V. is equipped with Internet access and it has the Amazon Prime app.

When you select this option you will get to a screen that shows you all of the available movies or T.V. shows that you can watch for free if you are an Amazon Prime member, or that you can rent to watch, like Netflix. This screen is divided into three sections if you are an Amazon Prime member, the shows that you can watch and access for free, movie rentals and T.V. shows to rent.

The Search field comes in handy on this screen if you are looking for a specific show or program to watch. You can also go to www.amazon.com and look at all of the available content there if you are more comfortable navigating on your computer.

Docs: When you select "Doc" this will bring up a list of all the documents that are on your Kindle Fire. To send documents to your Kindle you will be provided with an email address on this screen, and you simply send an email with an attachment to this address.

Apps: This section lists all of the apps that you own. When in this section you can select either the Cloud or the Device to see the apps that are yours. There is also a button on this screen to access the App Store on www.amazon.com. If you have downloaded an app previously and have not yet used it, the app will be listed on this screen.

Web: Selecting this option will bring up the Silk web browser. You can access most any web site using the Silk browser.

Section three of the home page: the carousel

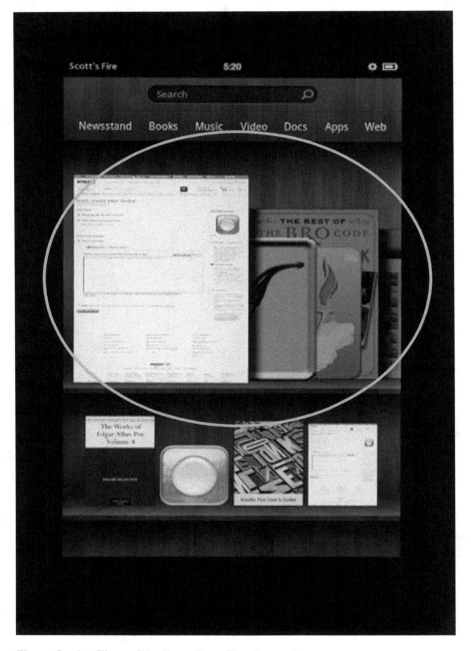

Figure Section Three of the Home Page: The Carousel

The third section of the hoe page is the carousel. This section contains a list of all the apps or books that you have recently read or used. It is an easy way to open up the latest book you are reading or opening up your favorite app that you happen to be playing. If you recently browsed the web a graphical icon will show up here as well.

To scroll through the carousel use your fingertip to swipe across the screen over the carousel section and this will rotate the selections. The faster you swipe, the faster the icons move across the screen.

To remove an icon from the carousel, simply tap the icon and hold your finger down on it. A menu will come up that will ask if you want to "Add to Favorites," "Remove from Carousel," or "Remove from the Device." Select the action you would like to perform by tapping on that menu bar. To escape from these options tap anywhere else on the screen.

Section four of the home page: the favorites.

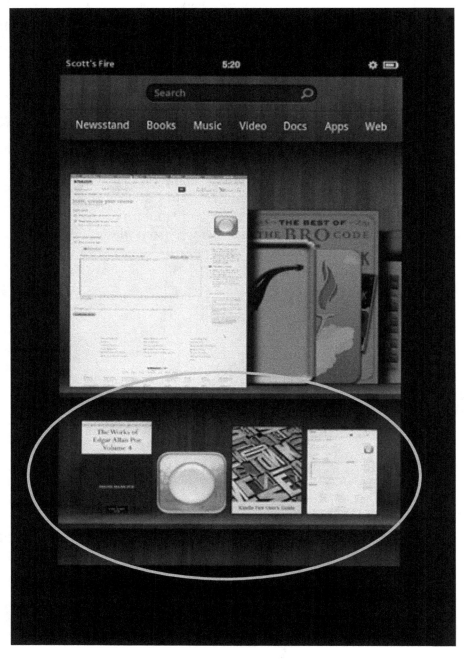

Figure Section Four of the Home Page: Favorites

The final section of the home page screen is the favorites section. This section on your screen can be the biggest, because when you add items to your favorites the Kindle will simply add another shelf if it needs more space. Thus, you can swipe your finger, in this section, from bottom to top and it will scroll down to the next shelf or shelves in your favorites. You can move icons up in your favorites section by lightly touching the icon and dragging it to the shelf that you want it placed upon.

To remove an icon from the favorites, simply tap the icon and hold your finger down on it. A menu will come up that will ask if you want to: "Remove from Favorites." Select the action you would like to perform by tapping on that menu bar. To escape from this option tap anywhere else on the screen.

5. The Kindle Fire Settings

The settings icon looks like a gear in the upper right hand corner of the Kindle Fire home screen. When you touch this gear six options come up: Lock/Unlocked, Volume, Brightness, Wi-Fi, Sync, and More. Most of these items are very easy to figure out but we will cover them all in this chapter.

Lock/Unlock: This tab will lock or unlock the screen rotation feature. If you do not want the screen to rotate with the direction you are holding your Kindle Fire, then simply set this option to "Lock." Unlock will allow the screen to rotate based on how you are holding your device.

Volume: This tab controls the master volume of the device.

Brightness: This tab controls the brightness of the Kindle Fire screen.

Wi-Fi: This tab will bring up the Wireless Networking screen. This screen displays all the wireless networks that are available to your Kindle at that time. To select your home network find it on the list and if you have a password for your home network then you will have to supply a password for the Kindle Fire.

The **Advanced Settings** option under the Wi-Fi tab will bring up another screen that will let you manually put in the following information: "IP Address," "Router," Subnet Mask," "DNS1," and "DNS2." This screen should only be used by advanced users who know all the settings of their router and network.

Sync: This tab will sync your Kindle Fire with the content that exists on your cloud drive. The Kindle must have Wi-Fi access to accomplish this.

More:

Under the **More** tab exists several more settings for the Kindle. These settings get used infrequently so they are a little harder to get to than the setting buttons for things you will use all the time. All of these settings will be discussed below.

Help and Feedback: This tab contains information and Kindle help topics, forms for sending feedback to Amazon and general customer service information.

My Account: This displays the account name that your Kindle Fire is registered to. You can either register your Kindle Fire here or you can deactivate your Kindle Fire here (if you ever wanted to sell your Kindle you would deactivate it here).

If you want to change the name of the Kindle Fire or you want to change the email address associated with this Kindle Fire, you can do this at www.amazon.com/myk. MYK stands for "Manage Your Kindle."

Parental Controls: This option allows you to control what content is available to your Kindle Fire. In order to use the parental controls you first have to create a password. Once you create a password, hit the finish button to bring you to the content you want to restrict. By selecting "On" next to the specific content, you will block access to that specific content on the Kindle Fire. For instance, if you do not want your child to download apps on the Kindle tap the "On" button next to the "apps" option under parental controls. When you choose to use parental controls, a lock icon will appear in the status bar.

Sounds: This option lets you control the volume of your Kindle Fire. You can also select a sound for incoming notifications.

Display: This option lets you control the brightness of your screen and it allows you to choose the number of minutes of inactivity before the Kindle Fire goes into sleep mode.

Security: This option is where you can put a password on your Kindle.

Applications: This option displays all of the applications you have installed on your Kindle. The default is to display all running applications on the Kindle Fire. You can filter the results by choosing either "Running Applications" or "Third Party

Applications" or "All Applications" from the dropdown menu.

You can select any application by tapping on the icon. Once in the options for the app you have chosen, you can uninstall the program from this point or you can change some options and permissions. Be sure to scroll up to view all the program information listed, including permissions.

Date & Time: This option allows you to manually set the date and the time on your Kindle Fire. If you want to, you can select "automatic" and the Kindle Fire will set this information for you.

Wireless Network: This option allows you to turn the wireless sniffer on or off. If this option is turned on it will display all available wireless networks in range of your Kindle Fire. You can also add a new network here and you can access the advanced wireless settings here.

Kindle Keyboard: This option lets you customize your keyboard behavior on your Kindle Fire. The customization you control is the "Sound on Keypress," the "Auto-capitalization" and "Quick Fixes," which automatically corrects commonly typed mistakes.

Device: This option contains all the information about your Kindle Fire. It shows you how much storage you have on the device for both applications and content (like music and books). This option also shows you how much battery life is left, the version of the Kindle Fire operating system you have installed, the serial number of your Kindle Fire, the Wi-Fi address, an option to control who can install applications on your Kindle and finally, a button that allows you to restore everything on your Kindle back to the factory defaults. This option should be used if you ever decide to sell your Kindle.

Legal Notices: This option displays all the legal jargon that comes with your Kindle.

Terms of Use: This option will connect you to a screen that does not work as of this writing. I would assume that this screen contains more legal information about your Kindle Fire.

6. Amazon Marketplace

Shopping for content for your Kindle fire is easy and extremely well-integrated to provide you with a hassle-free experience. You can either search for content on the Kindle Fire device itself or you can go to your computer and go to www.amazon.com to do your Kindle shopping. If you signed up for Amazon Prime you will get email notices about content that is free or on sale every week. There are always a lot of books available for free at any given moment and these free books can change daily. If you are a bibliophile I would check Amazon a couple of times a week to see if any new books are free.

Shopping for content on the Kindle Fire

In order for you to get content from Amazon using your Kindle Fire you must have Internet access and be hooked up through Wi-Fi. Each type of content has its own access point to get to the Kindle store online using your Kindle Fire. Each section will be covered independently.

The Newsstand

To get to the Amazon store for the Newsstand select Newsstand from the top menu item on your home screen. Once you select that, touch the "Store" button in the upper right-hand corner of the screen. You will then be connected to the Amazon Newsstand store.

At the top of the screen you will see all of the available newsstand items that have a 90 day free trial. You can scroll through all the options by using your finger and dragging it in the free offers part of the screen, from right to left, like you were turning the pages of a book.

The rest of the magazines and newspapers that are available to you are sorted by genres down below. You can scroll though all the genres by sliding your finger from the bottom of this portion of the screen to the top.

In the left column there are different links to browse all magazines, newspapers, interactive magazines, or the Kindle Book Store. You can also search for title by tapping your finger in the search bar on the top of the screen, which will bring up a keyboard for you to type in your request.

Books

To get to the Amazon Marketplace for books, touch the "Books" menu from the homepage and then touch the "store" button.

The top section contains books that are recommended for you based on books read or purchased from Amazon in the past. The books that Amazon recommends could be free and in the public domain or they could be books that they want to sell you.

The next section is labeled "Top 100 Paid." This is the Amazon Best Seller section in Amazon Marketplace and is a good indication of what is popular at the given moment.

If you scroll down far enough you will find the section called "Top 100 Free" which contains a large selection of books that are either in the public domain or books that publishers are offering for free in order to increase their book rankings in Amazon.

When you select a book to purchase it will bring up a screen that contains a synopsis of the book, suggestions of other books that were purchased by people who bought this book, and a button to download your book. If you have your credit card on file you will find it very easy to purchase and enjoy books.

Music

The music section in Amazon Marketplace is also divided into several different sections that make it easy to navigate. I personally do not use my Kindle Fire to play music because I love my iPod and the iPod is specifically designed to be a music player. Plus, my music would fill up the space on my Kindle Fire. While the Kindle Fire is large and relatively clunky to be a music player, the iPod family is built to travel.

The one great thing about downloading music from www.amazon.com is that it is downloaded as an mp3 file. These music files can be added to your iTunes library and Amazon seems to be very competitive in price with Apple iTunes. You will find specials all the time on Amazon.

If you want to purchase music on your Kindle Fire select "Music" from your homepage and then click on the "Store" link on the upper right-hand corner of the screen. The music store here is divided into several different sections showing the title available by Featured, Bestsellers, New Releases etc. You can also use the search window at the top of the screen to search for any song or artist.

To exit the Music store, click on the "Library" link at the top of the screen.

Video

The video store on Amazon shows you all of the movies or TV shows that available to purchase and view on your Kindle Fire. If you are a member of Amazon Prime, the first section of videos that appear are all the ones that are available to watch for free. There is a nice mixture of current and older movies as well as popular TV shows. When you select a video to watch, it downloads the video automatically and the video will be displayed in full screen mode, so you will have to turn your screen sideways.

Like all the other stores mentioned above you can see all the titles available in any subsection by selecting the "See more" link to the right of the genre.

My HDTV and my Blue Ray DVD player both have widgets that link to Amazon and allow me to access video content on my TV. If you are a member of Amazon Prime you will need to go into the widget and select a movie or TV show to watch. At this point you will be presented with a code and you have to log into www.amazon.com to enter the code into your account. This will link your Amazon Prime account with your TV or DVD player. Once you do this, the movies and TV shows that are free to watch will now appear in the listing from the widget.

The Kindle Fire has a nice screen and I have watched several movies on the Kindle. I also watch movies and TV shows on my HDTV. It is nice to have options, and I have found that the Amazon Prime membership tends to offer more free and current movies than my Netflix account does. If you sign up for Amazon Prime there is a good chance that you could quit your Netflix account and that would pay for your Prime membership.

Documents and file structure on the Kindle Fire

When you first select the "Documents" option on your homepage, you will enter to an empty bookshelf. On this screen there is the Kindle email account that is tied to your device. Different devices will have different email addresses.

There are two different ways to get documents on your Kindle Fire. The first is to buy a USB cable that will connect your computer to your Kindle Fire. To transfer files plug your USB cable into the Kindle Fire and plug the other end into your computer. The Kindle Fire will appear on your computer like any other USB connected device.

From your computer you can drag and drop different file types into the correct folder on the Kindle Fire. As long as you put the correct file in the correct directory on your Kindle Fire, it will appear after you move the files over to the correct folder.

The following file types are supported on your Kindle Fire:

Documents: AZW, TXT,PDF, MOBI, PRC, DOC, DOCX
Audio or Music Files: MP3, Non-DRM AAC (.m4a), MIDI, OGG, WAV
Images: JPEG, GIF, PNG, BMP
Video: MP4, VP8

The other way to get documents to your Kindle Fire is to send an email with an attachment to the email address on your Kindle Fire on the documents screen. When you send an email to your Kindle Fire, the Kindle Fire will automatically save the attachment as a document on your Kindle. You can then read the document, edit it, or otherwise treat it as a working document.

In order for you to be able to send attachments via email to your Kindle Fire you will need to ensure that the email address you are using will be accepted by the Kindle. You will need to go to your Amazon account online and log into your account. Go to www.amazon.com/myk.

On the left hand side of the screen, after you log in, you will see a section labeled "Your Kindle Account." Under this select "Manage Your Device."

Under the listing of all of your Kindles, you will see a link that says, "Personal Document Page." Select this and under "Approved Personal Document Email" select the option to add an email account. Add any and all email accounts that may send documents to your Kindle Fire.

Apps

To get to the App store select the "Apps" link from the top menu of your homepage. Once you are on the apps screen it will list all the apps that you own either on your device or on the cloud, depending on which tab you have highlighted on top. To get to the app store touch the link labeled, "Store." Inside the store there are many different categories of apps as well as listings for all the free apps available at the time. To purchase you must have an account set up with Amazon.

When most people think of apps they think of games. There are a lot of games available for the Kindle Fire but there are also some very nice productivity packages available. Make no mistake, the Kindle Fire as it is now will never be your computer workhorse; it just does not have the memory or power to do that. Thus most of the apps you will use will tend to be games or entertainment.

Shopping for content for your Kindle Fire via www.amazon.com

The other way to ship for content for your Kindle Fire is to do it via your computer through www.amazon.com. When you go here you can search for content for your Kindle Fire, including music, apps, books, and periodicals. When you purchase something this way, the next time you start your Kindle Fire the content you purchased will be available to you.

7. Surfing with Silk

Silk is Amazon's way to access the Internet. It is similar in function to Microsoft's Internet Explorer. Once you get the hang of browsing the web on a handheld device, Silk is an easy way to navigate your way through the web.

To open the Silk web browser simply tap on the "Web" link on the homepage of your Kindle Fire. It is near the top right hand corner. When you first access Silk it will come up with a list of recently visited web sites listed in grid format.

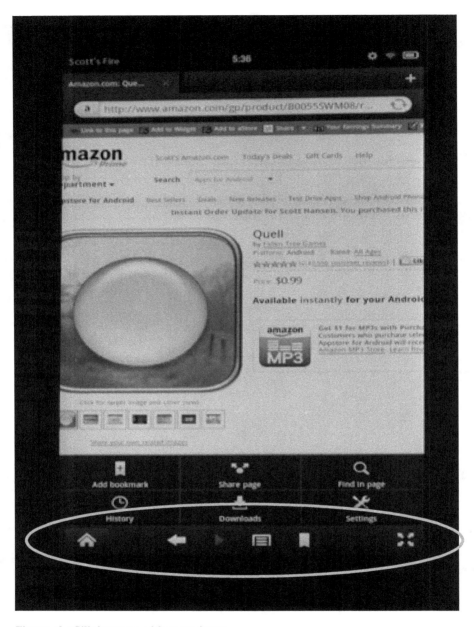

Figure the Silk browser with menu icons

The bottom section of the Silk browser contains a couple of different icons that are not used anywhere else in the Kindle Fire. To the right of the menu icon there is a bookmark icon. When you touch this icon a list off all the pages you have bookmarked will appear.

The icons in Silk

Bookmarks Icon: A bookmark in a web browser works the same way that a bookmark works when reading a book. It marks web pages that you have visited. If you visit a particular web site frequently you will want to bookmark the page which will save you the steps of typing in a web site's URL.

To bookmark a page type in the web site you want to bookmark. For instance, go to www.amazon.com. From the bottom icons select the menu icon, and this will bring up an extended list of icons from which you can choose. Select "Add bookmark" to keep track of this web site.

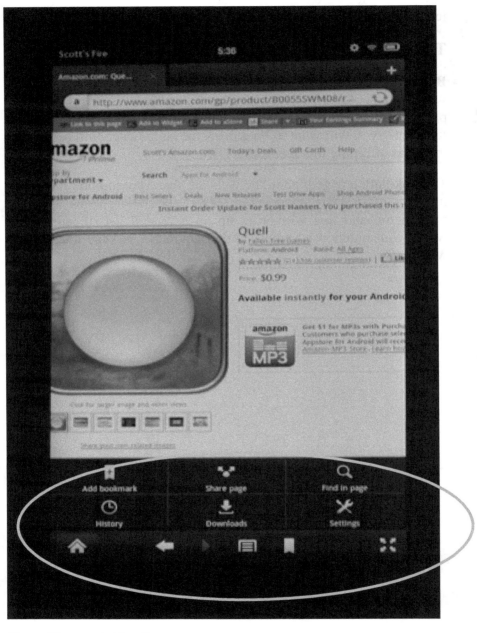

Figure The extended icon list

Let's say that you go to www.yahoo.com and you see a list of stories that are trending that day and you want to read one of them. Simply touch the link when it appears in the silk browser and it will take you to the article you want to read.

When you get to the page where the article is at, a new icon will appear to the right of the original bookmark icon and this icon is shaped like a pair of glasses. If you want to read the article like you would a book on the Fire, without all the Internet ads and links, simply touch the pair of glasses. The article you selected will now appear on a new screen and the behavior will be like a book. You can change the font size and scroll through the article with ease. It is an easy and well thought out way to read articles on the internet.

Share a page: The "Share a page" icon will bring you to a screen where you can log into Facebook. Use this icon to share any interesting articles with your friends on Facebook.

Find in page: The "Find in page" icon brings up the search bar on the top of the screen. Simply tap the search bar and then type in the words or phrase that you want to search for on this web page.

History: The "History" icon brings up a list of all the web sites you have visited. It is divided into five different sections: Today, Yesterday, Last 7 days, Last month, and Older. Tap on one of these headings to open up that section to display the web sites you have visited. To clear all your web browsing history tap on the "Clear All" button in the upper right-hand corner.

Your internet history is kept for 30 days before it is automatically deleted.

Downloads: The "Downloads" icon will display all of the downloads you have made to your Kindle.

Silk Settings: This icon will bring up a list of all the settings you can control with the Silk browser.

Silk's Settings

General

Set Search engine: When you select this option it will let you choose between Google, Bing or the Yahoo search engine.

Text size: This option will change the default text size when you use the Silk browser.

Default zoom: This option allows you to set the default zoom rate in the Silk browser.

Auto-fit pages: This option allows you to format the web pages to fit on the Fire screen.

Load images: This option asks if you want to display the images that exist on web pages.

Saved Data

Accept Cookies: This option asks if you will allow sites to save cookies and read them from your device. Cookies contain information that the web site you are visiting will use to remember you. Cookies may save login information about you so you do not have to fill in information every time you visit a web page.

Clear all cookie data: This option deletes all the cookies that are on your Kindle Fire.

Clear cache: This option clears the cached data stored on your Fire. Cached data is data about a web page that is stored locally on your Kindle Fire. This allows the web site to load quicker the next time you visit it.

Clear history: This option clears out the browser history.

Remember form data: Form data is information that you tend to fill out a lot when you purchase things on the web. This information is things like your name, phone number, address, and email address. When you go to fill out this information in the future, this data can be filled out automatically if you have this box checked.

Clear form data: This option clears out all the information from the form data. When you fill out information like your name, address, email, and phone number this information is stored on your Kindle Fire.

Remember passwords: This option will keep all passwords that you use for different web sites. I would set this to "off" in case your Kindle is lost or stolen.

Clear passwords: This option clears out all your saved passwords.

Behavior

Show security warnings: This option will display a security warning if there is an issue with a web site's security. You may not want to do business with web sites that do not have valid security certificates.

Enable Flash: This option allows you to enable Flash. Flash is animation software that allows you to view videos and play games.

Enable Java Script: Java Script is a programming language that allows certain programs to work on your Kindle.

Open pages in overview: This option displays an overview of all newly opened pages.

Open in background: If this option is checked it will open all new windows or links behind the current window that you have open.

Block pop-up windows: This option blocks pop-up windows to open when you navigate through the web.

Advanced

Accelerate page loading: This option will help load web pages faster in Silk. I have read that this does not work as advertised and if you turn this option off your web sites will load faster. Nonetheless I keep this option checked.

Optional encryption: This option will encrypt data you send from the Fire to the Silk servers when you have the acceleration pages checked. Encryption will slow down the data transfer but will "hide" or scramble your information to the rest of the internet world.

Desktop or mobile view: This option will let you choose to display website content either in desktop mode, or mobile device mode, or it will have the Kindle Fire automatically detect which version to use. A lot of popular web sites have scaled down web pages that will display better on mobile devices like cell phones. These web sites are not as pretty to look at as the normal web sites you visit on your computer.

Text encoding: This option allows you to change the language that your web sites display in. For instance, Chinese and Japanese languages use symbols instead of the Latin alphabet and if you want to read the web sites in Chinese you would change this option here.

Website settings: This option allows you to configure advanced settings for specific and individual web sites.

Reset to default: This option restores the default settings and you would use this if you were to go sell your Kindle Fire.

Downloading content: To download videos or images onto your Kindle Fire, press and hold the item and then tap the save option when it appears.

8. Email

With the Kindle Email app you can access many, if not all, of your other email applications and get and receive emails using your Kindle Fire. The main email program not supported is Microsoft Exchange.

To access the free Kindle Fire email app simply tap the "Apps" link from your homepage and then select the Email App icon. Once you hit the app icon you will enter the program. Select Start.

A list of email accounts supported appears in list form. These emails include Gmail, Yahoo, Hotmail, AOL and the venerable 'Other." Select which email program you use and then login to your email account. You will then be prompted to choose how you want your name displayed when you send outgoing emails, and you can also assign a name to the email account.

If you leave the "Send mail from this account by default" then anytime you use email on your Kindle Fire it will be sent through this account.

If you leave the "Import contacts" setting selected then all of your contacts in your email will be imported into the Kindle.

To see the contents of your inbox, touch the "View your inbox" button.

If your e-mail is not one of the ones listed above, then you will need to supply details about your account to the Kindle Fire. You'll need your password, login name, POP3 or IMAP port, and server settings to complete a manual setup. Amazon provides a nice little chart if your email account is not one of the ones listed above. To access it go   here: http://www.amazon.com/gp/help/customer/display.html?nodeId=200 830370. If your email is not listed in the chart above then you will need to contact your email provider.

Viewing your email

When you go to your inbox the first 25 emails are displayed. To see more emails scroll to the bottom of the screen and tap the "Load up to 25 more" icon.

The dropdown menu in the upper right hand corner allows you to sort your emails based on the following parameters: Newest, Oldest, Subject, Sender, Flagged, Read, Unread, and Attachments.

To read any email tap on it and it will open up. As usual, the back arrow will take you back one page, to your inbox, once you are done reading the email.

If you tap the menu icon (the one that looks like a piece of paper with writing on it) then you can select from "Mark as unread," "Move" or "Mark as spam" only while one email is open.

The email icons

The main mail icons are on the bottom of the mail screen app and are made up of the back arrow, the menu icon, the sync icon, the write icon and the search icon.

The back arrow icon: This icon will take you back to the previous screen

The menu icon: This icon will bring up a subset of icons that include: edit list, help, contacts, accounts, folders, and settings.

Edit list: Tapping this icon brings up all of your emails in list form with a check box next to it. You can select emails by tapping the check box. Once you select one or more emails then you are presented with the following options: Mark as unread, Move, Delete, or Done. This is the quickest way to manage a large number of emails.

Help: This option brings up the help content on mail.

Contacts: This icon will bring up all of your contacts associated with this email account. If you did not import any of your contact information you can now do it at this time or you can enter contact information one at a time.

Accounts: This icon will bring you to a listing of all your email accounts you have going to your Kindle Fire. If you tap the menu icon on the bottom of this screen you will be presented with the following options: Contacts, Add account and Settings. If you select contacts at this point you can add contacts. Adding account allows you to pull in more than one email account to your Kindle Fire. The stings option will bring up a check box to put the email app into debug mode.

Folders: The Folders icon will bring up a list of folders in your email app. If you go to this screen the first time it might be a blank page. Simply tap the blank page to bring up a list of your folders. The app will pull in all folders associated with your email account. There is no way to add a folder from the app. If you want a new folder here you must log into your email via the internet and add a folder there.

Settings: The Settings icon will bring up the settings in the email app. It is here you can really personalize the email application. Here is a list of the settings options:

Account Name: This assigns a name to any email account.

Default account: If you have more than one email account being loaded into your Kindle Fire you must select one to be the default email account. All emails sent from your Kindle will be sent from the one that has the "Default Account" item checked.

Always Show Images: The options here are No, From contacts or From anyone.

Fetch new messages: The options here are push or manual.

Sync server deletions: The options here are Do not delete on server, Delete from server or Mark as read on server.

When I delete a message: The options are Do not delete on server, Delete from server or Mark as read on server

Incoming server: If for any reason your email provider tells you to change the incoming server name or any other settings, this is the place you would do it. For the default email programs listed above, this screen should never have to be accessed.

Composition defaults: This screen holds the default information that will pertain to all emails you send out. It is here you can change your name as it is displayed, your email address, you can select someone to receive BCC (Blind carbon copy) on all emails going out, and you can select a signature.

Message format: You can select Plain text or HTML formatting.

Quote original message when replying: If this option is checked all emails you reply to will contain the original message in your reply.

Outgoing server: This option should only be changed if your email provider tells you to.

Archive folder: This option allows you to select a folder where all emails will go when archived. The default is left blank.

Drafts folder: This option allows you to select a folder where all draft emails will be saved.

Sent folder: Selecting this option allows you to select a folder where a copy of all sent emails will be saved.

Spam folder: This is the folder where spam emails go. If you have a spam folder on your regular email account you should never have to use this option because you are only pulling in emails from your inbox.

Trash folder: This option allows you to select where your trashed emails go.

The sync icon: Tapping this icon will make the app go check and see if there are any new emails in your email account.

The write icon: Tap this icon to create new emails.

The search icon: Tap this icon to search for names or phrases in your emails.

Deleting an email account in your Kindle Fire app: To deactivate an email account in your Kindle email app, tap the app to enter into your email inbox. When you select the back arrow a list of all the accounts that are being pulled into the application appears. Tap and hold the email account you want to delete until the account options screen appears. The bottom option on this screen is remove account.

9. Books, Books, Books!

The Kindle and the Kindle family of products are all about books. Books are the reason Amazon came into existence and books are the reason the Kindle was invented. With all that being said, if you want the best e-reader on the market you would be better off buying one of the other Kindle products that have a black and white screen. These Kindle's were designed to be e-book readers only and they have a screen that can be viewed in the light of a thousand suns. If you take one of the other Kindle's to the beach in Negril, odds are you will not be able to read any of the books you brought because the sun will be to bright. Besides that, the "ink" technology that they use with the other Kindle's is superb and it is easier on the eyes than the fonts and "ink" using the Kindle Fire. You cannot read books in a dark room on most Kindle models.

That being said, the Kindle Fire does a fine job for reading books provided the ambient light is not too bright. It is easy to purchase new books to read, it is easy to navigate through books you are reading, it is easy to make any adjustments you may want to make. If you are using the Kindle Fire as a reader you should have close to eight hours of battery life on a full charge. You can also read books in a dark room with no extra lighting needed.

Getting a book to your Kindle Fire is easy. You can either purchase or borrow books via your home computer or you can access the Kindle store using the Kindle Fire itself. You must set up an account with Amazon if you want to purchase books or join Amazon Prime if you want to enjoy the bonuses of free e-books and a vast lending library. Another option is a lot of public libraries have e-books that you can lend from them. Contact your local library for more information.

The books you own appear under the "Books" link on your homepage. Once on this screen select either "Cloud" or "Device" to see all the books you own. If you are going on vacation be sure to download any books you may want to read onto your device from the cloud in case you have internet connectivity issued on that remote island you will be visiting.

On your carousel you will notice that all books have a yellow ribbon in the upper right-hand corner with a percentage number on it. This percentage is how much of the book you have read. It is a convenient way to keep track of how far along you are in any given book.

Opening a book

To select a book go to your book link on the homepage. If you Have Wi-Fi connectivity you can read book directly from the Cloud, or you can go to the books on your device and read them from there. You will notice that some books may have a percentage label in the upper right hand corner of the book title, and this is simply telling you how far along you are in reading that book. To select a book to read, tap and hold your finger on the cover icon.

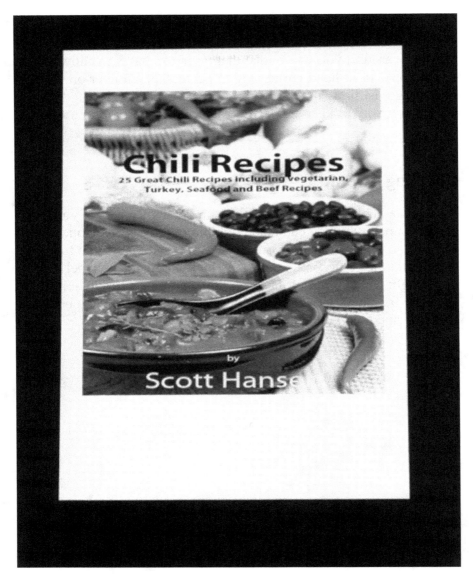

Figure An Amazon book...notice the author, who I have heard is a swell guy

When you tap on the book icon it will open up to the page that you last were reading. To turn a page in the book swipe your finger from the right hand side towards the left hand side of the Kindle Fire. To go back a page, swipe your finger from left to right.

The default action is to open your book in full-screen mode. You will notice the text covers the entire screen. There are no icons present. You cannot zoom in on a section of a page like you can on the web browser. To bring up all of the available icons tap anywhere on the screen.

When you do this the icons will appear at the bottom of the screen. The first item will be a visual representation of exactly how far along you are in the book. This is represented by a location diagram and a percentage next to the visual representation. If you want to jump further ahead or behind, put your finger on the slide bar and move it to where you want to go.

The next menu items are both new and familiar. They are: the back arrow, the font icon, the menu icon, the comments icon, and the search icon.

The back arrow: This icon takes you back to the previous action you made in the book. You can backtrack through several steps until you get to the point you were looking to find. This does not exit the book unless you use the arrow immediately after you enter in the book.

The font icon: This icon controls so much more than the font size. The wonderful thing about e-readers is that you can make the type as big or as small as you would like. If you do not want to wear the cheaters you can really increase the font size to a very large one. If you like more words on a page you can make the font smaller.

When you select the font size you will notice that you can select from two different tabs: the Font Style or the Typeface. If you want to change the actual font tap the Typeface tab and it will turn orange. You can select from eight different fonts.

When you select the Font Style tab you have several different choices. It is here you can control the size of the font, the line spacing in the book, the margins, and the color mode. The color mode allows you to change the color of the print from black to gray, or if you prefer you can change the background to black and they typeface to white.

The menu icon: When you tap the menu icon it will present you with several different choices. The options are: Cover, Table of Contents, Beginning, Location, Sync to Furthest Page, Book Extras and My Notes & Marks.

Cover will take you to the book cover.

Table of Contents will take you to the table of contents.

Beginning will take you to the beginning of the book, which in many cases is the same as the cover.

Location allows you to type in a location in the book where you want to go to.

Sync to furthest page will take you to the furthest point you have ever been in the book, but you will be asked if you really want to go there before it performs this action. Besides keeping track of where you left off the last time you read a book, the Kindle Fire also keeps track of the furthest place you have ever been in a book. Often times these are two different things.

Book Extras: connects you to the Shelfari community which is an encyclopedia for book lovers with content generated by the readers. It is sponsored by Amazon and here is the link: http://www.shelfari.com/. When you select Book Extras you will be brought to a page where you can add content about this specific book that will help other readers. You can add things like Plot Summary, Characters and Important People, Organizations, Glossary, Ridiculously Simplified Synopses, Themes and Symbolism, Classification, Errata, Quotes, Awards, First Edition, Settings and Important Places, Notes for Parents, Links to Supplemental Material, and Movie Connections.

If you download a famous book that is in the public domain, which is free by the way, and you go to the Book Extras under the menu icon, you will notice that most of them have the above information entered into them from other readers. There is a lot of great information contained in this section that many people will find interesting or useful.

My Notes & Marks: This option inactive unless you add your own notes inside of the book you are reading. If you have made comments or marks then they will all be listed in this section

Cool tools to use while reading a book

Highlighting a word or highlighting sentences: You can highlight a word by tapping on the word and holding your finger on it until a word is highlighted. To expand the highlighted section drag your finger from the starting point or the ending point of the highlighted section and then drag it until the sentence you want is highlighted. You may ask yourself, "Why would I want to do any of this?" There are a couple of very, very good reasons. You may not know a word and need a definition. You may want to highlight a word or sentences to come back to for future reference. You may want to search for the word or sentence in other places besides the book. You may want to share a great sentence or phrase with the rest of the world.

The Dictionary: Open a book on your Kindle Fire and then tap and hold your finger on a word. Immediately a dictionary will appear with the definition of that word along with a sub menu that includes: Note, Highlight, Share, and Search. The dictionary is an incredible tool that will give you the definition of any word in your book. You will no longer have to look up a word on the internet or in a dictionary. It is amazing.

Note: You can create your own virtual note next to any word or phrase that you want. When you do this a little note icon will appear next to the word or phrase you have created a note next to. This can come in handy if you want to remember to look up something at a later date.

Highlight: You can highlight a word or sentence by selecting the word or phrase you want to highlight, and then touch the highlight option after you have selected the word or phrase. When you select a word or phrase that you want to do more with, the word or phrase will stand out because it will be backlit with blue. If you do nothing and touch anywhere else on the screen the blue will disappear. When you highlight that word or phrase by selecting highlight, the word or phrase will be highlighted in yellow. It looks the same as highlighting information in a regular book.

Share: You must be connected to the internet for this option to work. This option will allow you to share a word or phrase with other readers of this book or on Facebook or Twitter.

Search: This option allows you to search for words or phrases in a book.

10. Magazines

There are two formats for reading magazines on the Kindle Fire (for most magazines). They are the Page View or the Text View. To select either of these views, tap on the screen when you open a magazine. When you do this the menu system will appear and you can choose either "Page View" or "Text View" on the top menu bar. Both versions have their pros and cons which will be discussed below.

The page view

There are some subtle differences between the Page View in magazines and how you read a book on the Kindle Fire, and this section will deal with those differences. When you select Page view the layout looks much like a magazine page with white space filling the top, bottom and sides of the article you are reading.

The biggest difference when using Page View is that the page behavior of magazines is the same as it is when using the silk browser. Unlike books, you cannot use the font icon to increase the size of the print on a page. However, you can zoom in on the text in a magazine like you can when surfing the web. To do this place your forefinger and thumb on the screen and pull your forefinger and thumb apart to zoom in. To zoom back out, place your forefinger and thumb, spread apart, on the screen and pinch them together while touching the screen.

To pull up the menu system while reading a magazine, tap anywhere on the screen. On the bottom, if you are in page view, you will notice the font icon is grayed out and not active. The available icons on the menu screen are: The home icon, the back arrow icon, the menu icon, and the search icon.

The home icon will bring you back to your Kindle homepage.

The back arrow icon will take you back one page, to the last screen you were on.

The menu icon will bring up the stories in the magazine. These act much like a chapter listing in a book. You can scroll through the different chapters by holding your finger on the screen and pushing up with your finger. To jump to a specific article, tap on it and you will go there.

The search icon allows you to search in the magazine for any words or phrases.

Finally, when you are in the menu system on "Page View" you will see on the bottom third of the screen, a snapshot of the pages that appear in the magazine. Use your finger to scroll through the pages and tap on any page to jump to that content.

The text view

The text view in the magazine section, allows you to read a magazine exactly how you would read a book using the Kindle Fire. When you choose the Text View the articles fill up the entire screen on your Kindle Fire. The articles behave exactly like they do when you read a book. You can change the size of the font using this option, and you can also change the spacing, the margins and the background colors.

When you have the magazine open and select Text View, tap on the screen and it will bring up the icon menu for you to use. Here you can select from these icons: The home icon, the back arrow icon, the font icon, the menu icon, and the search icon.

The home icon will bring you back to your Kindle homepage.

The back arrow icon will take you back one page, to the last screen you were on.

The font icon will bring up a sub-menu where you can choose the font size, the typeface, the spacing between lines, the margins on the screen and the colors used when reading. The behavior is exactly that when you read a book on the Kindle.

The menu icon will bring up the stories in the magazine. These act much like a chapter listing in a book. You can scroll through the different chapters by holding your finger on the screen and pushing up with your finger. To jump to a specific article, tap on it and you will go there.

The search icon allows you to search in the magazine for any words or phrases.

Also, immediately above the icons, there is an information screen which tells you what article you are currently reading as well as the length of the article in pages. You can also move easily to the next article by touching the forward arrow, or you can go back to a previous article by tapping the back arrow.

Magazines on the Kindle are easy to read and sometimes much cheaper than if you subscribe by mail. For a lot of publications you can only get the Kindle edition of the magazine if you subscribe to the paper form of the magazine. Some magazines are free through the Kindle.

It also helps that magazines can be customizable to make it easier for you to read them. Once you get the hang of using al the features you will love reading magazines on your Kindle Fire.

11. Music on the Kindle Fire

The Kindle Fire can be used as a music player, much like an Apple iPod. Personally, I do not use my Kindle Fire to hold my music because there is not a lot of memory available on the Kindle Fire and there is no way to expand it, and also because the iPod does music much better than the Kindle Fire.

That being said you can certainly use the Kindle Fire as a music player. The sound from the speakers is a bit tinny because the speakers are so small, but if you plug in a pair of headphones the sound becomes much better. Most likely, unless you are at home, you would want to wear headphones as to not disturb the people around you.

To get to the music section, tap the music tab on your Kindle homepage. The music screen is divided into two different sections, the Cloud and the Device. The Cloud contains all the music that is stored on the Amazon Cloud. The Device section contains all the songs that physically exist on your Kindle Fire.

The music icons

When you are in the music section of the Kindle tap anywhere on the screen and this will bring up the menu icons. The icons are: The home icon, the back arrow icon, the menu icon, and the search icon.

The home icon will bring you back to your Kindle homepage.

The back arrow icon will take you back one page, to the last screen you were on.

The menu icon will bring up three more icon options: The Downloads icon, the Settings icon, and the Help icon.
The Downloads icon: will bring you to the section that lists all your music downloads.
The Settings icon has these options: Enter a claim code, Clear cache, Lock-screen controls, Enable equalizer modes, Equalizer

mode (if Enable equalizer mode is checked), delivery preference, Automatic downloads, and Refresh Cloud Drive.

Enter a claim code: This option allows you to enter a gift card or promotional code.

Clear cache: This option will clear out any song information, album art, and the Now Playing queue.

Lock-screen controls: This option lets you use playback controls when your Kindle Fire is locked.

Equalizer enabled: This options turns on the equalizer if checked. The equalizer allows you to change the "sound" of a song.

Equalizer Mode: This option allows you to select from ten different equalizer modes: Normal, Classical, Dance, Flat, Folk, Heavy Metal, Hip Hop, Jazz, Pop, and Rock.

Delivery preference: This option lets you choose between saving your music on your Kindle Fire or saving the music on the Cloud. If you are going to use the Kindle Fire as a music player it would make sense to store you music on the cloud because of space limitations on the device.

Automatic Downloads: This option, if checked, will download all of your music purchases that are saved to the Cloud Drive down onto the Kindle Fire.

Refresh Cloud Drive: This option will update the music that appears on your cloud drive when you select Cloud. The Kindle Fire automatically updates this information every 10 minutes.

The search icon will bring up the search window. If you select this you can search on artist names, song titles or albums.

The tabs

The tabs in the music section are: Playlists, Artists, Albums, and Songs. The last three tabs are self-explanatory; they will list your music in alphabetical order by the tab you choose. Playlist is the tab we will discuss further.

Playlist: This tab allows you to create your own playlist or it allows you to view your music by the two default playlists: Latest Purchases or Latest Uploads. The last two playlists you have no control over, they are automatically populated by Amazon.

To create your own playlist, tap on "Create new playlist." This will bring up the keypad and a box asking you for the playlist name. Once you create the name of your playlist all of your songs will now appear in list form. To add songs to the list tap on the plus sign to the right of the song title. You can scroll through the songs like you scroll through the rest of the Kindle menus. Once you select a song to add to your playlist the song will be grayed out on the screen.

To search for a song on the Cloud tap inside the box labeled, "Search your Cloud Drive music." This will bring up the keypad and allow you to search by song title or artist.

Once you have your playlist set up, the next time you go into the music section you will see your playlist on the main screen if the "Playlist" tab is highlighted. When you tap on it to select it, it brings up a list of all the songs in your list. On the bottom of that screen you will see the standard play, forward one song or back one song icons next to the name of the song that will be played. Tap the play icon to hear your song.

Although the Kindle was not designed to be a music player, it does function fairly well in that regard. The icons are intuitive and it is easy to learn and master the controls. I would highly recommend that you purchase a nice set of headphones or ear buds if you want to listen to your music on your Kindle fire.

12. Video and the Kindle Fire

The Kindle Fire is a great machine to watch video on. The screen is large enough where the picture looks good, and if you put in a pair of headphones the sound is pretty good. The speakers generally work well with the video option. When you select the video tab from the homepage, you will enter a screen that looks much like the books screen. At the top you can select to view video either on the cloud or your device. I would not put any purchases on your device because video simply takes up too much room.

At the bottom of the screen are your icons. They are: The home icon, the back arrow icon and the menu icon.

The home icon will bring you back to your Kindle homepage.

The back arrow icon will take you back one page, to the last screen you were on.

The menu icon will bring up three more icon options: The Settings icon, the Your Watchlist icon, and the Help and Feedback icon.

The Settings icon: The Settings icon brings up the following options: Disable HD purchase warning, Disable non-Prime purchase reminder, clear search history, Device ID, Version, and Help & Feedback.

Disable HP purchase warning: The default is to warn you when you are purchasing HD videos. On the Kindle Fire you do not really need HD to get a nice picture. Thus, the default is to tell you if you are purchasing HD content.

Disable non-Prime purchase reminder: The default is to warn you if you are purchasing something that does not come free with your Amazon Prime membership.

Clear Search history: Clears the search history for videos on the Kindle Fire.

Device ID: The Device ID is a unique number that is assigned to your Kindle Fire. This cannot be changed.

Version: The version contains the version number of your Kindle Fire and cannot be changed.

Help & Feedback: This option brings you to the help screen. From here you can search the Frequently Asked Questions, or FAQ's, Contact Customer Support or leave feedback.

The Video Store: To access the video store tap on the Store icon in the upper right-hand corner. This will bring you to the Amazon Store and it is here you can rent or purchase videos. You can also stream free content if you are a member of Amazon Prime. I cannot recommend Amazon Prime enough. Besides getting free two day shipping on anything your order from Amazon.com (with no minimum purchase required), you also get access to free books and free videos.

The Video Store is divided into different sections. The first section is Amazon Prime. This area will list all of the free content available to you if you are a member. Hit the see more icon to get a full listing of what is available. Once you tap "See more" you will be presented with two tabs at the top of the screen, Movies or TV. Under each of these options is Popular Movies (or TV Shows), Recently Added, Editor's Picks, All Genres, and For the Kids.

There is also a search bar at the top of the screen which when tapped, will bring up a keyboard and allow you to search movies or TV shows by title, themes, or stars of these shows. It is a very useful feature.

Once you find a program you want to watch, tap on the icon of that show and you will be sent to the purchase screen. It is here you can watch the TV shows or movies that you purchased. Tap on the correct title for TV show episodes, or tap "Watch Now" next to the movie cover.

Remember, if you are a member of Amazon Prime, you can get an app for any device, big screen TV's, DVD players, etc. that will allow you to watch Amazon content on your TV. The app is not as well designed as the Netflix app, but once you start using it you will become familiar with it very quickly.

The Watchlist

The Watchlist is your wish list of shows you want to watch. I have found it easier to go online to www.amazon.com and look for movies or shows you want to watch. Once you find something that piques your interest then you can click on the movie or TV show icon and then instead of watching it instantly, you can tap the "Add to Watchlist" icon. This will add the specific TV episode or movie to a list of shows you want to watch. The next time you use your Amazon Prime app on your TV or DVD player, you can select the Watchlist option and a listing off all the shows you want to watch will be there.

The Watchlist is phenomenal. If you think about a show or movies you want to watch it is easy to find it and add it to your Watchlist, even if you are not near your TV. It works better than writing a note to yourself and when you are ready to watch a show or TV, you will have a ready list of shows that interest you. I use the Watchlist feature a lot, and it really is a nice feature in the Video section.

13. Top Apps for Kindle Fire

The thing to remember is by the time you read this book there will be many new games or apps out there on the market. The following are a list of some of the top games and apps that you can get for your Kindle Fire. I have played or used many of them, but I also went to the Amazon App store and found the top free and paid for games and apps. This is my current list of favorites.

Free Games:

1. Quell. This is another simple yet very addictive game. It is free, fun, easy to learn and harder than hell to master.
2. Angry Birds. Free and a paid version. I think everyone on the planet knows about this game by now so I will not write much about it at all.
3. Temple Run. Free. This is an addictive and relatively easy game to play. You are being chased by creatures and must run away from them traversing walls, jumping through the air and collecting gold coins.
4. Flow Free. A puzzle game where you connect matching colors with the same colored pipe. This game is addictive as well.
5. Garfield's Dinner. This game is very highly rated and seems to be geared for kids. Garfield the cat is in the kitchen and they are trying to run Irma's diner and fun ensues. This will usually only run in standard definition on your Kindle Fire because of memory issues.

Paid Games

1. Sherlock. This game is simple and addictive. You can get a trial version for free or pay $3.99 for thousands of different puzzles. This is my go-to game when I am bored or killing time.
2. Cut the Rope. A very addictive game where you cut swinging ropes to control the travel of sweets being fed to a monster, albeit a cute monster!
3. Angry Birds. Who doesn't love angry birds and when you pay you skip the ads!

4. Plants vs. Zombies. This game requires you to grow a garden and keep the zombies away from getting you! My daughter loves this game.
5. Amazing Alex. This is a puzzle game from the makers of Angry Birds. Turn the toys that Alex owns into anything!

Useful Apps:

1. Alarm Clock. Free. This app turns your Kindle Fire into an alarm clock which can be very useful when you are away from home.
2. Calculator Plus Free. An easy to use calculator that keeps track of items you have calculated which makes it a great tool to balance your checkbook, or it can be used to add up travel receipts.
3. Battery HD. This tool helps to keep track of the battery life left on your Kindle Fire. This breaks down how much battery life you have left while performing a specific task, like listening to music or reading books, or even watching videos.
4. Cozi Family Organizer. Cozi makes an app to connect to the Cozi web site which has many tools you can use to keep track of things happening in your family. The Cozi calendar is a fantastic tool that can email you when you have upcoming appointments.
5. File Manager for Kindle. Using this very useful tool you can manage or browse all the folders on your Kindle Fire. This tool allows you to open, delete, rename, or move files.
6. Avast Mobile Security. This powerful anti-virus software will keep your Kindle Fire free from viruses and it will protect your Kindle Fire by installing a firewall and a GPS tracking feature in case your Kindle is lost or stolen. I am not sure if the GPS tracking would actually work on a Kindle (unless they can figure out a location based on Wi-Fi locations) but the security features are top-of-the-line.
7. Netflix. If you have a Netflix account you can watch movies or TV shows on your Kindle Fire using this app. This is an excellent app to use with your Netflix account because the Kindle Fire was built with video in mind.

14. Troubleshooting

The best place to look for answers to your Kindle problems is the Internet. Simply go to Google and type in the issue you are having. For instance, "books not opening in my Kindle Fire." This will bring up multiple sites that have the answers and the first ones usually point to the Amazon web site.

There are two very important tips I can give you if you are having issues with your Kindle Fire. The first is to make sure your Kindle Fire is charged fully. This takes about four hours to complete when the battery symbol is on low.

The next piece of advice is to perform a hard reset. You do this by holding the power button to turn the device off for about 15-20 seconds. You will be successful when the unit turns completely off. I have done this several times to fix any Wi-Fi issues I was having as well as when I had issues opening books. The next time you turn your Kindle Fire on, the issues you were having should be resolved.

I also ran into Wi-Fi issues with my Kindle after not having any issues for months. This is extremely frustrating and I do not know if it is because of a Kindle Fire firmware update, or what, but I know things do not change without reason when it comes to computers. When I selected Wi-Fi is showed me as being connected to my network but there was an "x" next to the Wi-Fi symbol in the upper right hand corner of my screen and I could not get to the internet.

The first thing I tried was to do a hard reboot on the Kindle Fire. This means I held in the on/off button for about 20 seconds when turning my Kindle off. The first time my Wi-Fi had issues this fixed the problem. During this particular instance this first step did not work for me.

Next, I called Kindle for technical support and they suggested I take it to a Wi-Fi hotspot to see if I could connect to the internet. I went to my neighbor's house and they gave me the password to their Wi-Fi and I had no issues connecting to the internet. I noticed that I was using WPA-2 and WPA-Personal as my encryption key on my wireless network. My neighbors were using WEP security (which is less secure). I change my modem to use WEP security and put in the new password in my Kindle Fire and I can now connect to the internet. I did not find this information on any chat board in the internet, but I know this worked for me.

If all else fails here are the contact phone numbers for Kindle Technical Support. Inside the United States: 1-866-321-8851. Outside the United States: 1-206-266-0927.